Table of Contents

Introduction	4
Chapter One	6
What is a Golden Visa?	6
Chapter Two	8
The Golden Visa, a win-win formula	8
What are the differences between a Golden Visa and other kinds of permit to be found in the country?	*9*
Advantages of the Golden Visa:	*10*
Chapter Three	15
Golden Visa Investment Requirements	15
General Requirements:	*15*
Specific requirements regarding investment capital:	*18*
Chapter Four	21
Golden Visa Application Process	21
The process in a nutshell	*21*
Chapter Five	23
Frequently Asked Questions about the Golden Visa:	23
Conclusion:	28

Introduction

This is meant to be a guide for individuals, couples or families who are seeking to purchase property in Barcelona or the wider province of Catalunya, though details laid out in this guide apply across all of Spain. This book aims to provide a clear understanding of the obligations and conditions attached to purchasing a property and obtaining the coveted Golden Visas as a desired outcome after the purchase. While thorough and accurate at the time of writing, this guide is not a substitute for legal advice nor exhaustive in scope. If and when you are ready to set out on your own path to property ownership and residency rights in Spain, you are strongly encouraged to contact a qualified real estate agency and law firm within the desired jurisdiction.

Buying property abroad is an exciting prospect but the uncertainty surrounding rights, perks and obligations can be stressful and prohibitive. Conventional knowledge indicates that foreign buyers and prospective residents in a foreign country do not enjoy the same level of protection as provided to natural citizens, hence the understandable apprehension. Any concerns or doubts you therefore harbour, are perfectly normal and the reason we wrote this introductory guide to buying in Spain. We hope it's helpful and will set you on your way to owning a piece of paradise!

Chapter One

What is a Golden Visa?

The Golden Visa is a law put together by the Spanish legislature in order to encourage and boost the growth of the economy across the country. The law stipulates that any individual who meets certain administrative requirements and in addition also makes a minimum, fully committed investment of 500,000 euros is offered a quick way to obtain residency, with the further possibility to apply for permanent residency and even citizenship after a specific period and subject to separate requirements and applications.

A major perk of the Golden Visa is that it enables you - and if relevant and subject to further conditions - your family to travel freely across some twenty-six European countries that have signed on to be part of Europe's Schengen Area. The Schengen Area is an area consisting of European states that have officially abolished passport

Foreword

Like many people, I have spent a great deal of my life wondering which place I would choose to live in if I could choose any place in the world. Criteria such as quality of life, cost of living, access to world class healthcare, a great education for children, natural beauty and amazing food are usually on everyone's list when considering new horizons and exciting adventures. Spain, and especially the coastal area known as the Costa Brava all the way down to the region's capital city, Barcelona, has all of these desirable features and more.

As a natural born EU citizen I had to right to pack up from my native Belgium and simply move down to what I consider paradise. But what if you're not a EU citizen? Should you bury the dream of owning a rustic country estate or a luxury apartment, or indeed a beautiful villa on the coast? Should you abandon the idea of living in a relatively stress-free society, rich with culture, culinary delights and a fascinating history?

Can you live in paradise too and come and go as you please? The answer is an emphatic yes, YES YOU CAN!

I hope this guide will help you weigh your options and set you on a path to ownership and residency in Spain.

You can email me on ceo@buypropertybarcelona.com with any questions, we are always happy to serve.

Marc Mekki, co-founder of The Ode to Joy Collection

Copyright © 2019

All rights reserved. No portion of this book may be reproduced, stored in a retrieval system, or transmitted in any form or by any means – electronic, mechanical, recording or otherwise – except for brief quotation in printed reviews without the prior written permission of the publisher or the author.

Disclaimer

This document does not provide legal advice and does not create an any legal or commercial relationship or obligation on the part of the author or reader. Facts about visas, residencies, rights and regulations are subject to frequent change and some information contained within this document may be, though verified at the time of writing, no longer be accurate or complete. If you need legal advice, please contact an attorney directly.

and all other types of border control at their mutual borders. The area mostly functions as a single jurisdiction for international travel purposes, with a common visa policy. With the Golden Visa you'll have unrestricted access and wouldn't need to apply for a visa to visit these countries. It also allows you to live in Spain, and by consequence in semi-autonomous regions like Catalunya and its capital, Barcelona.

The primary appeal of the Golden Visa process is that it does away with the unnervingly complex red tape and bureaucracy that usually accompanies application for residency in Spain. Simply put, your Golden Visa gets you right to the front of the line, guaranteeing that you and your family do not have to go through the stress of standard residency application. And you'll own a beautiful property in the process!

Chapter Two

The Golden Visa, a win-win formula

The global financial crisis of 2008 was a major catalyst in the advent of Golden Visa programs across Europe. Desperate for economic rejuvenation and foreign investment, an increasing number of countries have drafted legislation to fast-track residency for investors in property, bonds and companies. In fact, by 2015, more 25% of the world's countries were offering Golden Visas in one form or another.

By the end of 2016, more than 2700 Golden Visas had been granted in Spain alone, making it the leading EU country in the granting of Golden Visas, overtaking Portugal.

Initially the law was known as the Investor's Residency Law. In 2013, the bill was passed into law paving the way for nonresidents of European Union countries to acquire residency visas and permits.

What are the differences between a Golden Visa and other kinds of permit to be found in the country?

1. Unlike every other permit, the Golden Visa does not require the applicant to stay or have stayed in the country for a specified length of time. You retain the right to come and go as you please, even if that is only sporadically. You're under no obligation to live in Spain once your Golden Visa has been issued.

2. The ease with which the Golden Visa is obtained cannot be matched by any other permit procedure. Once the applicant meets the investment requirements and submits a compliant dossier, the Golden Visa process can often be completed in as little as 20 days, though one to two months is more realistic since the process does not only involve the State's scrutiny but also the required preparative work by your appointed real estate agent and lawyers.

3. The Golden Visa grants the applicant the right to bring along their immediate family members as they are usually covered under one Golden Visa. There is no need to obtain a separate permit for the spouse or children.

Advantages of the Golden Visa:

Before you begin the process of applying for the Golden Visa you'll want to know all the benefits you accrue as a resident under this particular scheme:

1. As already pointed out, the Golden Visa path is mostly straightforward and quick. Attracting investment without hurdles or aggravation results in more applications and thus more income, so every effort is made to make sure the process is easy for you as a buyer. Also, the regulations and administrative requirements are quite clear and concise. The investor does not need to go through great lengths

to understand what is expected of him or her before he begins the Golden Visa process.

2. There is no requirement to become physically resident in Barcelona, Catalunya Province or indeed the country as a whole: you are expected to visit the country just once to apply for your residency permit, open a bank account and sign the deed on your new property (and other, minor practical tasks). Upon successful completion of the Golden Visa process a one year residence permit is issued. Once the first year permit expires you will be granted a two-year residency permit that is renewable every two years. You'll need to retain the services of a local lawyer for each renewal but this process is both quick and easy. Eventually, a path to permanent residency and even full citizenship may open up, with the potential to settle and work in other EU countries.

3. Subject to additional paperwork, approval and surcharges, the visa comes with the added benefit of granting your underage children (18 years old or younger at the time of application) the opportunity to travel and study across Europe, not just in Spain. As parents, you do not even need to take up physical residence for your children to be granted the right to live and study in Europe. For example, children can be issued with a European Student Card. This enables them to easily and safely identify and register themselves electronically at higher education institutions within the EU when moving abroad for studies, eliminating the need to complete on-site registration procedures and paper work

4. Subject to additional paperwork, approval and typically, surcharges, the visa comes also with the added benefit of granting your parents the

opportunity to enjoy the privileges of the same residence permit so long as they can be shown to be dependent.

5. Your property purchase may end up being a very profitable investment in its own right. Spain is experiencing a boom across its real estate sector with wealthy, accessible and prosperous parts of the country, such as Catalunya, at the forefront of this boom. This is a good time to invest in the real estate sector in Catalunya and make very compelling returns in the process, thus safeguarding your investment.

As a matter of fact, the country has experienced a double digit expansion in almost all the regions of the country. Your Golden Visa may very well end up being a golden investment too, further boosting its incredible appeal. But no one knows how long this particular path to residency in Europe will last, so if you're at all considering an investment, make enquiries as soon as you're ready.

Chapter Three

Golden Visa Investment Requirements

General Requirements:

There are several requirements laid down in the legal act which a buyer-investor must comply with before being granted the Golden Visa:

- The first requirement is that the person must be a non-EU national. The Golden Visa is primarily open to nationals of countries that do not form part of the European Union.

- The individual must be of legal age, i.e. the person must be at least 18 years of age.

- No criminal record in Spain or countries lived in during the last 5 years for offenses stipulated under Spanish Law. The law also states that the applicant must not be listed as 'objectionable' in the territorial space of countries with which Spain has signed an agreement in this regard.

- The buyer and any eligible family members applying for a Golden Visa must have comprehensive medical insurance with sufficient coverage to ensure no burden is placed on Spain's social health care system. The insurance can be of a private nature or a public/government sponsored one, so long as it sufficiently covers the applicants.

- The buyer-investor must have sufficient and demonstrable economic means to support himself or herself and his or her family for the entire time they are physically present in the country. This requirement is typically a non-issue because an individual who has the means to apply for the Golden Visa in the first place should definitely have the means to take care of his or her family. Still, a buyer should make an effort to set aside ample liquidity to demonstrate that sufficient financial means are no issue. The official government requirement at the time of writing this guide: minimum 2.130€ monthly for yourself and 532€ for every family member that is in your care. It is highly recommended not to take these amounts too literal as increases without notice are possible and all applications are individually scrutinised in any case.

- The party must pay the necessary fees demanded. Since there is no practical, feasible way for buyers to submit and process Golden Visa applications independently, the submission will be processed by qualified lawyers in Spain, and ideally in Barcelona. Fees can vary wildly depending on which legal firm one engages so it is worth shopping around or simply asking your real estate broker or consultant to point you in the right direction as they will know the lay of the land and will make sure you are suitably assisted.

Specific requirements regarding investment capital:
Apart from the general requirements, there are specific requirements that the investor must fulfil before being granted the Golden Visa. These requirements are mostly regarding the minimum monetary investment the buyer must commit to before being considered for the visa.

The individual seeking to obtain the Golden Visa needs to invest at least 500,000 euros in Spanish real estate property. It is important to understand that this amount must be committed in full and cannot, even partially, be comprised of a mortgage, other loans or any kind of debt financing, whether private, institutional or otherwise. For the Golden Visa to remain valid during subsequent renewal cycles, it is also critical that the invested amount does not drop below the initial 500,000 euros. Finally, this minimum investment excludes all related taxes and encumbrances such as lawyer fees, agency commissions, banking fees, transfer tax, VAT or any other expenses incurred as part of the buying and application process. It is therefore safe to assume that your financial capabilities should well exceed the cost of the property itself. Bear in mind that you must be able to demonstrate a legitimate source of funds as applications must pass anti-corruption checks, anti-money laundering checks and other audits. Another interesting fact is that the 500,000 euros minimum investment can be distributed between a number of different real estate purchases, if the buyer chooses to do so. But this will certainly complicate the entire process as well as inflate the overall cost. Common sense indicates that for most buyers, investing in a single property is by far the preferred option for the sake of simplicity and expedience. For investments that exceed the 500,000 euros threshold it is perfectly acceptable to fund the additional cost through a mortgage or other debt financing.

Chapter Four

Golden Visa Application Process

The process in a nutshell

Before you begin the Golden Visa process, you need to have begun making the required investments or at least need to have shown through deliberate action a complete willingness and intent to commit to the investment. In practice, this means that you must show evidence that the money required for the investment has been deposited in a bank in Spain. This deposit does not equate to an irreversible commitment at this stage, but it's the minimum requirement to be able to proceed.

Once your property purchase has been completed, you will be required to submit to your chosen local law firm a straightforward dossier comprising of the following documents:

- documented proof of the investment,

- valid foreign passport,

- NIE (Foreigner's Identification Number); required to sign deeds and fulfil a range of other administrative tasks,

- confirmation of sufficient economic means to cover personal and family living expenses,

- public or private health insurance authorised to operate in Spain;

- certificate confirming no criminal record whether in Spain or in the country of residence,

- marriage certificate, children's birth certificate (if the family members obtain a resident visa).

Your lawyer will process and submit the necessary paperwork to the government. This process takes about 20 days. You are not even required to return to Spain after the approval is granted; your lawyer can forward the permits to your home address overseas.

Chapter Five

Frequently Asked Questions about the Golden Visa:

1. Do I need to take up physical residence in Spain or Catalunya to comply with Golden Visa residency regulations?

Under any other residency statute such as student visas, work permits and other residency permits, it is typically required to have a physical presence in the country. Golden Visa holders however are exempt from such conditions and are allowed to live outside of the country while holding a residence permit. That exemption is one of the factors that make the Golden Visa so attractive to foreign non-EU buyers. Only during the initial stages of the process is the applicant required to visit Spain, and only once. It is therefore perfectly possible to enjoy Spanish residency and all of its perks while still living outside of Spain.

2. Will the Golden Visa afford me the opportunity of traveling freely within the European Union?

Yes, individuals who have the Spanish residence permit associated with a successful Golden Visa application are allowed to enter freely into all European countries that are part of the Schengen area without the requirement of a visa, for up to 90 days at a time out of every 180 days.

However, the individual has to bear in mind that not all European countries are part of the Schengen Agreement. Countries such as the United Kingdom, Ireland, Croatia, Monaco and a host of others aren't part of the agreement and therefore will not grant automatic access to Golden Visa residency holders. Most of the major European economies are part of Schengen however. For a map overview, please visit: http://bit.ly/SchengenCountriesEurope

3. Can I work in Spain under a Golden Visa?

A residency bestowed as a result of a successful Golden Visa application automatically grants the successful applicant the right to take up employment in Spain or start a business. However, this only applies for individuals who hold a valid Golden Visa residence permit *and* reside in Spain for a minimum of 183 days per calendar year. This as opposed to permit holders who may still enjoy the privileges of a Golden Visa but who may not take up employment or start a business. Once a Golden Visa residency holder resides in Spain for more than 183 days per calendar year, they are considered residents, which in addition to holding the rights to work and start a business also introduces the obligation to pay taxes and obtain a local identification number, known as a N.I.E. (Número de Identidad de Extranjero).

4. *Does the Golden Visa expire? If it does, is there an option for renewal?*

The first residence permit granted is granted for a period of one year, after which the buyer-investor can seek to extend it for another two years. Subsequent two-year extensions can be granted indefinitely. The only requirement is that the applicant would continue to maintain the minimum level of investment required. While obtaining a Golden Visa can eventually allow successful applicants to apply for permanent residency and even citizenship, keep in mind that these procedures are entirely separate from the Golden Visa residency and therefore in no way is an applicant guaranteed a successful outcome of a permanent residency or citizenship application after five or ten years are respectively.

5. Would my income be taxed when I invest in Catalunya to obtain the Golden Visa?

An investor only gets taxed on their worldwide income if they stay in Catalunya for more than 183 days of the year. For others who aren't resident in the country or don't reach the 183-day threshold, tax is charged (at a rate of 24% at the time of writing this guide) on all of the income derived in the country, including rental income, regardless of whether or not the Golden Visa holder is physically present.

Conclusion:

Spain's popular Golden Visa policy has opened up compelling investment and relocation opportunities for individuals and families willing to take the plunge. Cities like Barcelona and the wider Catalunya region offer robust housing markets, an excellent quality of life and increasingly, startup business opportunities.

Having read through this guide on the benefits of obtaining the Golden Visa, only one question remains:

When are you buying your place in paradise?

For further reading and updates, please visit:

www.buypropertybarcelona.com

or email the author on:

ceo@buypropertybarcelona.com

www.ingramcontent.com/pod-product-compliance
Lightning Source LLC
Chambersburg PA
CBHW031940170526
45157CB00008B/3261